Born Hungry

Julia Child
Becomes "the French Chef"

Alex Prud'homme   Illustrated by Sarah Green

CALKINS CREEK

AN IMPRINT OF ASTRA BOOKS FOR YOUNG READERS

New York

Julia McWilliams wore size twelve sneakers, stood six feet, two inches tall, played basketball, laughed loudly, and was curious about everything. All this activity made her crave food—*lots* of food.

But Julia's parents had a cook—and Julia only knew how to boil water and make toast. "I was never encouraged to cook and just didn't see the point in it," she said.

"I was born hungry, not a cook."

Julia always dreamed of having adventures and becoming a famous writer. When America joined World War II, she volunteered for the US spy agency, the Office of Strategic Services (OSS). The OSS sent her to Ceylon (now Sri Lanka), an island country near India, where she worked as a clerk typist, helping spies, soldiers, and generals with their top secret reports.

But Julia was a little bit lonely.

One day in 1944, Paul Child moved into the office next to Julia's. She could see him through a little window. A painter and photographer, he was ten years older than she was, several inches shorter, and much quieter.

"We had such fun!"

Paul had lived in Paris and knew all about food and wine. In the OSS, he designed maps, charts, and a secret war room for the generals. Julia did not like his mustache. Paul thought she was too loud. But they both liked food, books, and travel.

Soon, she encouraged him to take an elephant ride in the jungle, and he encouraged her to try foods from around the world.

Julia still did not know how to cook, but, in the OSS, she created her first recipe—for shark repellant. Sharks would try to bite US sailors or would accidentally blow up US sea mines.

Julia used copper acetate mixed with black dye to create a small, round "cake" that smelled like dead shark. When it was submerged, the cake disintegrated and the repellant spread through the water, scaring hungry sharks away.

After the war ended, Julia and Paul moved back to America and married.

"With a new husband...I decided I'd better learn to cook."

Julia Child signed up for a class on how to make pancakes and hamburgers. But when she cooked her first meal for Paul, Julia tried something more complicated—cow brains simmered in red wine! "It sounded exotic and would be a fun way to impress my new husband," she told herself. But she rushed through the recipe and admitted that her dinner was "a disaster." They ate cheese and crackers instead.

Julia grew determined to learn how to cook well.

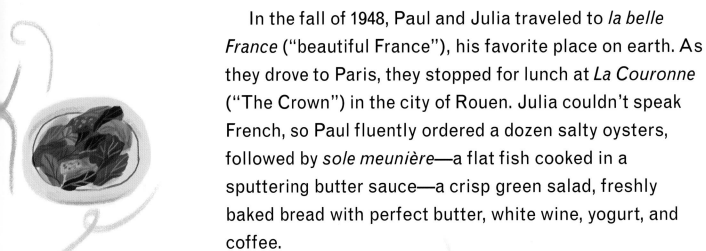

In the fall of 1948, Paul and Julia traveled to *la belle France* ("beautiful France"), his favorite place on earth. As they drove to Paris, they stopped for lunch at *La Couronne* ("The Crown") in the city of Rouen. Julia couldn't speak French, so Paul fluently ordered a dozen salty oysters, followed by *sole meunière*—a flat fish cooked in a sputtering butter sauce—a crisp green salad, freshly baked bread with perfect butter, white wine, yogurt, and coffee.

As the waiter carefully laid their plates on the table, he smiled and said,
"Bon appétit!"
"Enjoy your meal!"

Julia inhaled the wonderful aroma of fish cooked
in butter. Then she took a bite of the sole, experienced
"a magnificent burst of flavor," and closed her eyes. She
had never tasted anything so fresh and delicious.
She tried to chew slowly, to savor every morsel, but the
lunch was so good that she gobbled it down.

"yum!"

Mopping her plate spotlessly clean with the bread, Julia sat back and sighed, wondering if *she* could ever make such a feast.

"It was the most exciting meal of my life!"

In Paris, Paul worked at the US embassy while Julia consumed food of every kind—sweet pastries, cold zucchini soup, roasted pheasant, steak, lobster, snails, frogs' legs, potatoes in cream sauce, green beans with lemon, wild mushrooms, eggplant and tomato stew, cheeses of every description, light lemon tarts, dense chocolate cakes, and plump strawberries swimming in pools of whipped cream.

"yum!"

Every night before bed, Julia read French cookbooks for fun. She fantasized about making a "poem of poached and flavored sole fillets surrounded by oysters and mussels, and napped with a wonder-sauce of wine, cream, and butter." But it still took her hours to make dinner, and her meals were often missing something.

After a year in Paris, thirty-seven-year-old Julia decided it was high time she learned how to properly cook a French meal. "I had so much more to learn, not only about cooking, but about shopping and eating and all the many new (to me) foods," she wailed. "I wanted to roll up my sleeves and dive into French cuisine."

"I hungered for more information!"

Julia signed up for classes at the famous Le Cordon Bleu cooking school—the only woman in a class of American soldiers studying in France after World War II. They did not want a tall, loud woman in the kitchen. But Julia became the hardest worker and best student. Every day, she woke up eager to get back to the stove.

Chef Max Bugnard taught Julia to cook simple dishes, like *oeufs brouillés* (scrambled eggs), and more complicated ones, like *boeuf bourguinon* (beef stew).

"How does it *taste*, Madame Child?" Chef Bugnard asked, sipping the stew. He added a touch of salt and pepper, tasted it again, and when the flavors were just right, he grinned.

And he always would say, "Cooking is joy! Cooking is fun!"

"yum!"

Julia learned to dice, fold, marinate, poach, purée, and sauté. She could whip up a bowl of *vichyssoise* (a cold leek and potato soup), or roast a delicious dinner fit for a queen, like *oie rôtie aux pruneaux* (goose with prune and *foie gras* stuffing).

Her favorite desserts were *tarte Tatin* (a caramelized apple tart) and *gâteau reine de Saba* (a chocolate and almond cake).

"yum!"

"yum!"

Chef Bugnard took Julia shopping in Paris's outdoor markets. He pointed out that if she wanted the tastiest cut of meat, the freshest loaf of bread, or the gooiest piece of cheese, she would have to "take *time* and *care*" to talk to the butcher, baker, or cheese maker. Talking to people was one of Julia's favorite things to do, and she was good at it.

"She could charm a polecat," Paul said. Julia loved "the people, the food, the lay of the land, the civilized atmosphere, and the generous pace of life."

When Julia and two French friends opened *L'École des Trois Gourmandes* ("The School of the Three Hearty Eaters"), Julia taught her students the lessons she had learned from Chef Bugnard:

"Good results require that one take *time* and *care*. If one doesn't use the freshest ingredients or read the whole recipe before starting, and if one rushes through the cooking, the result will be an inferior taste and texture. . . . But a careful approach will result in a magnificent burst of flavor, a thoroughly satisfying meal, perhaps even a life-changing experience. Such was the case with the *sole meunière* I ate . . . on my first day in France."

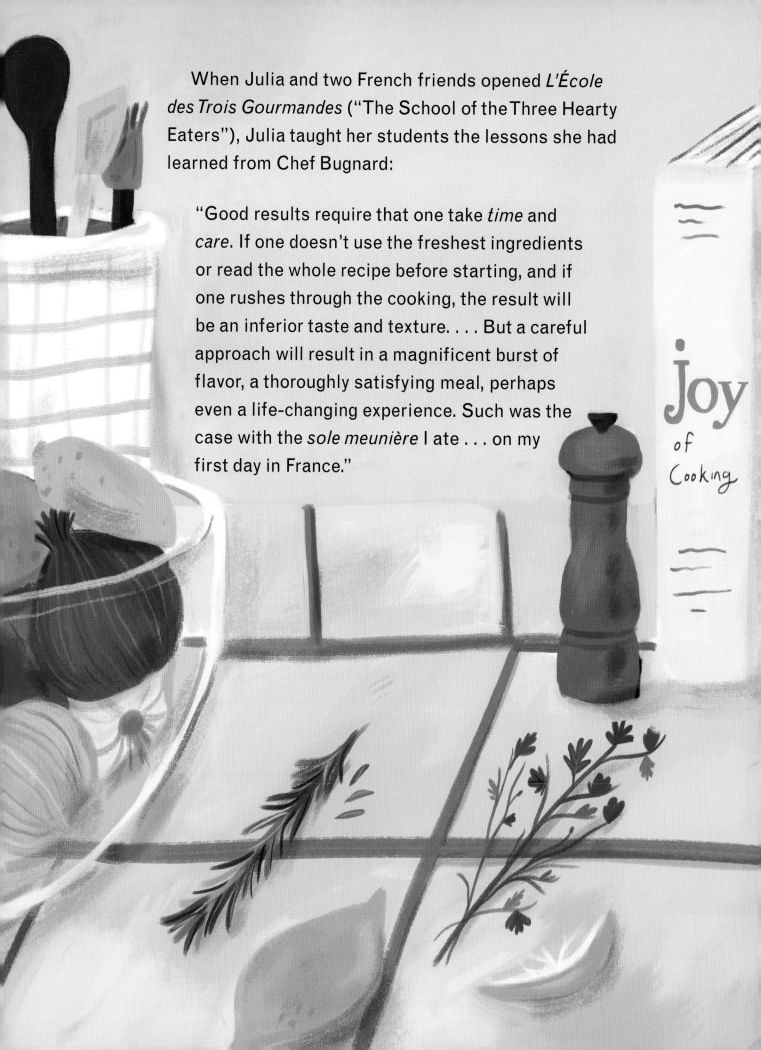

Julia Child encouraged her students to work hard—to use the best tools, to take risks, to never apologize for cooking mistakes, and—more than anything—to have fun!

AUTHOR'S NOTE

"Find something you're passionate about and stay tremendously interested in it."

Julia Child holding two big boules, a French type of bread

In 1961, Paul and Julia Child retired from diplomatic service and settled in Cambridge, Massachusetts, outside Boston. They planned to live a quiet life. He would paint and take photographs, while she would write and teach cooking. That October, Julia published her first cookbook, *Mastering the Art of French Cooking*. She hoped people would be interested, but she worried, "Will anyone buy our book?"

At the time, many Americans ate cheap foods from cans and boxes, which required little effort to make or clean up. Julia's book had the opposite message: it is far more satisfying to take the time and care to make a delicious meal from healthy ingredients.

"Besides," she would say, "cooking is *such fun*!"

The cookbook had taken seven years for Julia and two French friends to write. It was 750 pages long and had been rejected three times by American publishers. "It's too complicated!" they grumbled. "We want to cook something quick, with a mix!"

Hearing that, Julia worried that all her hard work had been a waste. But then a young editor named Judith B. Jones realized that Julia's book was unlike any cookbook that had been written before. Judith convinced her boss, Alfred A. Knopf, to publish *Mastering the Art of French Cooking* in October 1961. The book sold well (it has never gone out of print) and changed Julia's life.

In 1963, a public television station asked Julia to host a cooking show called *The French Chef*. Though she didn't own a TV set at the time, she was a natural performer. Combining years of cooking experience with a zesty sense of humor, she demonstrated how to make a delicious French onion soup, a veal casserole, and baked apples. Then she'd accidentally burn her finger, spill a bowl of flour, or smear her cheek with chocolate sauce. When that happened, she'd tilt her head back and laugh.

At the end of every episode, Julia would say, "Bon appétit!" And she meant it.

Millions of people across the country tuned in to watch *The French Chef*. Julia was smart and funny, made silly mistakes, but also taught her audience how to make a mouthwatering dinner in half an hour. She encouraged viewers to demand better meat and vegetables from their markets; buy good knives, pans, and stoves; and try ambitious recipes.

She told people not to be afraid of rich food: "If you don't like butter," she joked, "use cream." And: "Everything in moderation, including moderation."

If a dish failed, Julia advised, "Never apologize! One of the secrets of cooking is to correct something if you can, and bear with it if you cannot. Maybe the cat has fallen into the stew, or the lettuce has frozen—too bad! The cook must simply grit her teeth, bear it with a smile, and learn from her mistakes."

By 1967, Julia had won an Emmy Award and a Peabody Award, had appeared on the cover of *Time* magazine, and was the first person to take TV cameras into the White House kitchen.

In 1973, Julia left *The French Chef*, began performing as "Julia Child," and used recipes from around the world—New England baked beans, Italian pasta, Belgian chocolate, Indian curry. She expressed her opinions about politics,

diets, and culture. Her outspokenness brought her attention as well as criticism. But Julia just laughed and kept doing what she loved to do.

In 1980, she left public television to cook on *Good Morning America*, a commercial TV show, where she found a bigger audience than ever. That year, Julia turned sixty-eight years old and became America's first, true celebrity TV chef.

Over her career, she wrote fourteen books, hosted eleven cooking shows, and won many awards, including the Presidential Medal of Freedom, America's highest civilian honor. For a complete listing of her many awards, see juliachildfoundation.org.

Julia Child died in her sleep on August 13, 2004, two days before her ninety-second birthday. At the time, I was helping her write a memoir about her favorite years of her life, when she and Paul lived in Paris and Marseille (1948 to 1954), and she learned to cook. Her memoir, *My Life in France*, was published in 2006, became a best seller, and in 2009 inspired half the movie *Julie & Julia*.

Today, more Americans than ever consider themselves "foodies," and Julia Child is one of the major reasons why. She was a revolutionary who taught America to cook with a smile.

Paul Child and Julia in France

Julia Child and her teacher Chef Max Bugnard

THE ESSENTIAL JULIA

BOOKS

1961: *Mastering the Art of French Cooking*
(By Julia Child, Louisette Bertholle, and
Simone Beck)
1968: *The French Chef Cookbook*
1970: *Mastering the Art of French Cooking*, Vol. II
(By Julia Child and Simone Beck)
1975: *From Julia Child's Kitchen*
1978: *Julia Child & Company*
1979: *Julia Child & More Company*
1989: *The Way to Cook*
1991: *Julia Child's Menu Cookbook*
1993: *Cooking with Master Chefs*
1995: *In Julia's Kitchen with Master Chefs*
1996: *Baking with Julia* (Julia Child with Dorie
Greenspan)
1999: *Julia and Jacques Cooking at Home*
(Julia Child and Jacques Pépin)
2000: *Julia's Kitchen Wisdom: Essential
Techniques and Recipes from a Lifetime in
Cooking*
2006: *My Life in France* (Julia Child with Alex
Prud'homme)

TV SHOWS*

1963–1973: *The French Chef*
1978–79: *Julia Child & Company*
1979–80: *Julia Child & More Company*
1983–84: *Dinner at Julia's*
1993: *Julia Child & Jacques Pépin: Cooking in
Concert*
1993–94: *Cooking with Master Chefs*
1994–96: *In Julia's Kitchen with Master Chefs*
1995-96: *Julia Child & Jacques Pépin: More
Cooking in Concert*
1996–98: *Baking with Julia*
1999–2000: *Julia and Jacques Cooking at Home*
2000: *Julia's Kitchen Wisdom*

*Most of these shows, and several compilations of
The French Chef episodes, are available on DVD or for
streaming on the PBS website, pbs.org.

PODCAST

"Inside Julia's Kitchen," hosted by Todd
Schulkin, Executive Director of the Julia Child
Foundation for Gastronomy and the Culinary
Arts
To listen: juliachildfoundation.org
To subscribe: iTunes, Stitcher, Spotify

WEBSITES*

The Julia Child Foundation for Gastronomy and
the Culinary Arts: juliachildfoundation.org

Julia Child and Paul Child Papers at the Arthur
and Elizabeth Schlesinger Library on the
History of Women in America
To visit: Radcliffe Institute for Advanced Study,
Harvard University, 3 James St., Cambridge,
MA, 02138
To visit online: Julia Child | Radcliffe Institute
for Advanced Study at Harvard University:
radcliffe.harvard.edu/schlesinger-library/
collections/julia-child-2

Alex Prud'homme's website:
alexprudhomme.com

*Websites active at time of publication

EXHIBIT

Julia Child's Kitchen at the Smithsonian

Julia Child's kitchen, which was originally in her home in Cambridge, MA, is on display at the Smithsonian's National Museum of American History in Washington, DC.

To visit: the National Museum of American History, 1300 Constitution Avenue, NW, between 12th and 14th Streets, Washington, DC 20560

To visit online: americanhistory.si.edu/food/julia-childs-kitchen

BIBLIOGRAPHY

All quotations in the book can be found in the following sources.

Child, Julia with Alex Prud'homme. *My Life in France*. New York: Alfred A. Knopf, 2006.

Personal conversations between Julia Child and Alex Prud'homme.

Prud'homme, Alex. *The French Chef in America: Julia Child's Second Act*. New York: Alfred A Knopf, 2016.

Prud'homme, Alex, and Katie Pratt. *France Is a Feast: The Photographic Journey of Paul and Julia Child*. New York: Thames & Hudson, 2017.

TEXT AND PICTURE CREDITS

Julia Child image, photograph, & related rights™ © 2020 The Julia Child Foundation for Gastronomy and the Culinary Arts: 39.

Photograph by Paul Child © Schlesinger Library, Radcliffe Institute, Harvard University: image no. olvwork539043: 36; image no. 8000982822: 37; image no. olvwork581328: 38.

Text permission (p. 40): "Oeufs Brouilles (scrambled eggs)" from MASTERING THE ART OF FRENCH COOKING, VOLUME 1 by Julia Child, Louisette Bertholle, and Simone Beck, copyright © 1961 by Alfred A. Knopf, a division of Penguin Random House LLC. Used by permission of Alfred A. Knopf, an imprint of the Knopf Doubleday Publishing Group, a division of Penguin Random House LLC. All rights reserved.

The three friends—Louisette Bertholle, Julia Child, and Simone Beck (left to right)—cook fish at L'Ecole des Trois Gourmandes.

To Hector and Sophia —AP

To my mom, a Julia fan and lover of cookbooks —SG

Text copyright © 2022 by Alex Prud'homme
Illustrations copyright © 2022 by Sarah Green
All rights reserved. Copying or digitizing this book for storage, display, or distribution in any other medium is strictly prohibited.

For information about permission to reproduce selections from this book, please contact permissions@astrapublishinghouse.com.

Calkins Creek
An imprint of Astra Books for Young Readers, a division of Astra Publishing House
calkinscreekbooks.com
Printed in China

ISBN: 978-1-63592-323-0 (hc)
ISBN: 978-1-63592-560-9 (eBook)
Library of Congress Control Number: 2021906335

First edition
10 9 8 7 6 5 4 3 2 1

Design by Barbara Grzeslo
The text is set in Grotesque MT.
The illustrations are done digitally.

SCRAMBLED EGGS*
[Oeufs Brouillés]

Scrambled eggs in French are creamy soft curds that just hold their shape from fork to mouth. Their preparation is entirely a matter of stirring the eggs over gentle heat until they slowly thicken as a mass into a custard. No liquid or liquid-producing ingredients such as tomatoes should be beaten into them before cooking, as this is liable to turn them watery.

Please ask an adult to help you.

For 4 or 5 servings

A fork or a wire whip
8 eggs, or 7 eggs and 2 yolks
A mixing bowl
¼ tsp salt
Pinch of pepper

Beat the eggs in the bowl with the seasonings for 20 to 30 seconds to blend yolks and whites.

2 Tb softened butter
A heavy-bottomed, enameled, pyrex, earthenware, or stainless steel saucepan or skillet 7 to 8 inches in diameter. Depth of eggs in pan should be ⅔ to 1 inch.
A rubber spatula, wooden spoon, or wire whip

Smear the bottom and sides of the pan with the butter. Pour in the eggs and set over moderately low heat. Stir slowly and continually, reaching all over the bottom of the pan. Nothing will seem to happen for 2 to 3 minutes as the eggs gradually heat. Suddenly they will begin to thicken into a custard. Stir rapidly, moving pan on and off heat, until the eggs have almost thickened to the consistency you wish. Then remove from heat, as they will continue to thicken slightly.

1½ to 2 Tb softened butter or whipping cream
A warm buttered platter
Parsley sprigs

Just as soon as they are of the right consistency, stir in the enrichment butter or cream, which will stop the cooking. Season to taste, turn out onto the platter, decorate with parsley, and serve.
(*) The eggs may be kept for a while in their saucepan over tepid water, but the sooner they are served the better.

Tb = tablespoon
tsp = teaspoon